ALASKA

by Joyce Johnston

Lerner Publications Company

You'll find this picture of a mountaintop at the beginning of each chapter in this book. Alaska boasts not only the highest peak in the United States—Mount McKinley—but the next 15 highest peaks as well. More than a million tourists each year come to Alaska to experience the outdoors and enjoy the majestic scenery.

Cover (left): Totem pole at the Totem Heritage Center and Nature Park in Ketchikan. Cover (right): Sled dog team in the Iditarod race. Pages 2-3: Inside Passage near Sitka. Page 3: Grizzly bear in Denali National Park.

This book is available in two editions:
Library binding by Lerner Publications Company, a division of Lerner Publishing Group
Soft cover by First Avenue Editions, an imprint of Lerner Publishing Group
241 First Avenue North
Minneapolis, MN 55401 U.S.A.

Website address: www.lernerbooks.com

Library of Congress Cataloging-in-Publication Data

Johnston, Joyce, 1958–
    Alaska / by Joyce Johnston. (Revised and expanded 2nd edition)
       p.   cm. — (Hello U.S.A.)
    Includes index.
    ISBN: 0–8225–4051–7 (lib. bdg. : alk. paper)
    ISBN: 0–8225–4157–2 (pbk. : alk. paper)
    1. Alaska—Juvenile literature. [1. Alaska.] I. Title. II. Series.
    F904.3 .J64 2002
    979.8—dc21   2001000326

Manufactured in the United States of America
1 2 3 4 5 6 – JR – 07 06 05 04 03 02

CONTENTS

The Last Frontier

"ush!" That's what some dogsled drivers yell to start their dog teams down a snow-covered trail. Because Alaska is as far north as you can go and still be in the United States, you might think that the state is nothing but endless snowy trails in a land of ice and cold. But Alaska is also a land of rain and fog, mighty mountains, steaming volcanoes, and colorful plants and animals.

Alaska is the largest state in the United States. More than twice the size of Texas, Alaska is known for its vast wilderness. The state has almost 200 national and state parks, forests, and other areas protected by the government.

Cotton sedge grows in Alaska's marshy areas.

7

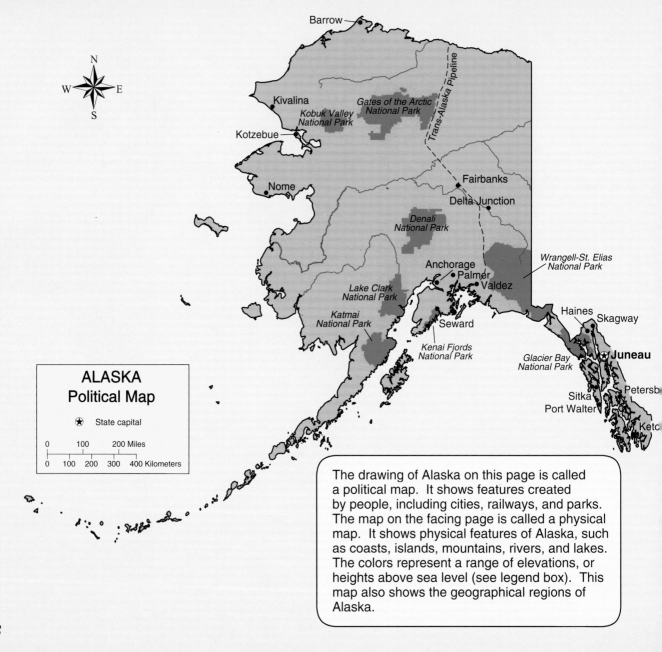

ALASKA
Political Map

⊛ State capital

0   100   200 Miles
0 100 200 300 400 Kilometers

The drawing of Alaska on this page is called
a political map. It shows features created
by people, including cities, railways, and parks.
The map on the facing page is called a physical
map. It shows physical features of Alaska, such
as coasts, islands, mountains, rivers, and lakes.
The colors represent a range of elevations, or
heights above sea level (see legend box). This
map also shows the geographical regions of
Alaska.

Barrow

N
W   E
S

Kivalina

Kobuk Valley
National Park

Gates of the Arctic
National Park

Trans-Alaska Pipeline

Kotzebue

Nome

Fairbanks

Delta Junction

Denali
National Park

Wrangell-St. Elias
National Park

Anchorage
Palmer
Valdez

Lake Clark
National Park

Haines
Skagway

Katmai
National Park

Seward

Kenai Fjords
National Park

Glacier Bay
National Park

☆ **Juneau**

Petersb

Sitka
Port Walter

Ketc

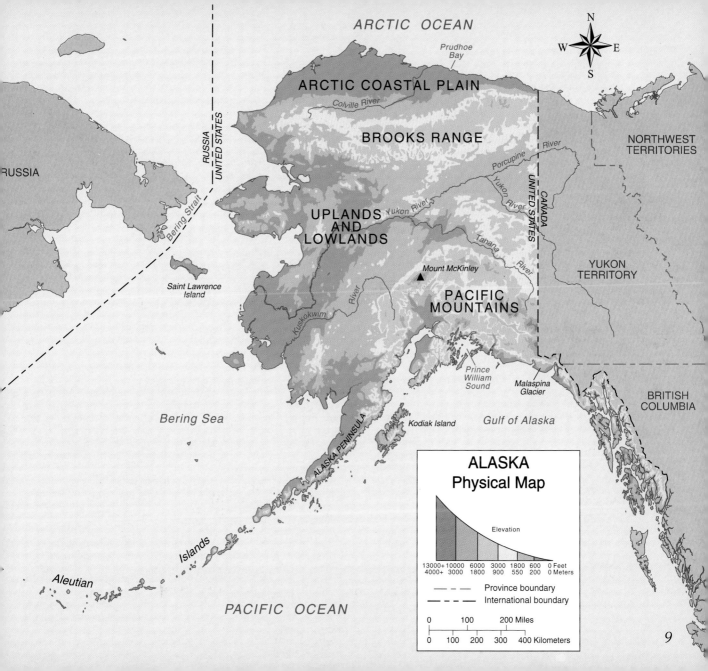

ARCTIC OCEAN

W N E S

Prudhoe Bay

ARCTIC COASTAL PLAIN

Colville River

BROOKS RANGE

RUSSIA

UNITED STATES

RUSSIA

Bering Strait

Saint Lawrence Island

River

Porcupine River

Yukon River

NORTHWEST TERRITORIES

UNITED STATES

CANADA

UPLANDS AND LOWLANDS

Yukon River

Tanana River

YUKON TERRITORY

▲ *Mount McKinley*

PACIFIC MOUNTAINS

River

Kuskokwim River

Prince William Sound

Malaspina Glacier

BRITISH COLUMBIA

Bering Sea

Kodiak Island

Gulf of Alaska

ALASKA PENINSULA

Aleutian

Islands

PACIFIC OCEAN

ALASKA
Physical Map

Elevation

| 13000+ | 10000 | 6000 | 3000 | 1800 | 600 | 0 Feet |
| 4000+ | 3000 | 1800 | 900 | 550 | 200 | 0 Meters |

– – – Province boundary

– – – International boundary

0   100   200 Miles

0 100 200 300 400 Kilometers

9

Like the island state of Hawaii, Alaska is not physically connected to the rest of the United States. The Pacific Ocean, the Canadian province of British Columbia, and Canada's Yukon Territory separate Alaska from the 48 mainland states. Alaskans call the mainland states the Lower 48.

Water forms most of Alaska's borders. The Gulf of Alaska and the stormy Pacific Ocean lie south of the state. To the west are the Bering Sea and the narrow Bering Strait. North of Alaska is the icy Arctic Ocean. These bodies of water are home to whales, fish such as salmon and halibut, and many types of shellfish. Sea otters, fur seals, and many seabirds live along the coast.

Alaska has four land regions. They are stacked on top of one another from south to north. The Pacific Mountains make up the southernmost region,

Fur seals leave Alaska each winter for the warm waters of Mexico, thousands of miles to the south.

topped by the Uplands and Lowlands region, the
Brooks Range, and the Arctic Coastal Plain.
Altogether, Alaska's four regions are shaped like a
square kite with two tails.

   The two tails are part of the Pacific Mountain
range. One tail drifts west into the ocean from
Alaska's southwestern corner. It includes a
peninsula called the Alaska Peninsula and a chain
of islands called the Aleutian Islands. The other tail
drops from Alaska's southeastern corner. Made up
of islands and a narrow strip of coast, this tail is
known as the Alaska Panhandle.

On the Alaska
Peninsula, the lakes
and rivers teem
with fish.

Mount McKinley is so steep and difficult to climb that only about half of the climbers who have tried to scale it have made it to the top. American Indians call the mountain *Denali,* which means "great one" or "high one."

Many rugged mountain chains wrinkle the landscape in the Pacific Mountain region. These ranges are part of the Coast Ranges—a mountain system that extends down the Pacific coast of North America as far as southern California. One of Alaska's peaks, Mount McKinley, pokes through the clouds at 20,320 feet—higher than any other mountain in

A portion of the border between Alaska and Canada is marked by a strip of land that has been cleared of trees.

North America. Large white sheep called Dall sheep climb the hillsides of the Pacific Mountains.

The biggest region in Alaska is the Uplands and Lowlands. Low hills separate the region's wide, swampy river valleys. Alaska's longest river, the muddy Yukon, winds all the way across this region, from the Yukon Territory in Canada to the Bering Sea. Several of Alaska's other major rivers—including the Kuskokwim, Tanana, and Porcupine—also flow through the Uplands and Lowlands region.

The Brooks Range is home to abundant wildlife, including gray wolves *(left)* and grizzly bears *(below)*.

The area around the Yukon River is home to reindeer and musk ox. About 80 percent of the world's emperor and Canada geese nest there in the summer.

Alaska's Brooks Range is the northernmost arm of the Rocky Mountains, a chain that extends southward through Canada and the Lower 48 as far as New Mexico. The Brooks Range is Alaska's most untamed land region, and few people live here. Caribou, moose, wolves, porcupines, and grizzly bears roam through the region's wildlife preserves and wilderness areas.

In the regions covered by permafrost, melting snow never soaks into the frozen ground.

The flat Arctic Coastal Plain lies north of the Brooks Range. Also called the North Slope, the plain gradually drops from the foothills of the Brooks Range to the Arctic Ocean. Only the top few inches of soil on the Arctic Coastal Plain thaw in the summer. Because the soil below is always frozen, the ground is called **permafrost.** The Colville River and other waterways in the region thaw for only about 10 weeks every summer.

Alaska's climate is as varied as its landscape. Along the southern coasts and islands, the weather is mild and very wet. Every year, Port Walter on the Alaska Panhandle receives about 220 inches of rain and melted snow—more than anywhere else in the United States, except Hawaii.

Farther inland, away from the coast, the climate is dry and the winters are long and very cold. About 13 inches of **precipitation** fall yearly. Winter temperatures can drop as low as −70° F. But during the short summers, temperatures sometimes rise above 90° F.

Along the Arctic coast, even the summers are cool. The average July temperature in this part of the state is only 47° F. Just 8 inches of moisture fall here each year.

Deep snow covers some parts of Alaska.

Beautiful hiking trails wind through Alaska's national parks.

Alaska's long, cold winters are brightened by frost-covered red leaves like these.

Summer on the Arctic Coastal Plain brings a brief display of hot-pink fireweed, blue forget-me-nots, and many other kinds of wildflowers. There are no trees on the coastal plain, but the state's other regions are heavily forested. Western hemlock, birch, Sitka spruce, and white spruce trees all grow in Alaska.

THE HISTORY

From Land Bridge to Land of Gold

Across the Bering Strait, just 51 miles from Alaska, lies a part of Russia called Siberia. Long ago, a bridge of dry land crossed the Bering Strait, linking Siberia to what later became Alaska. During that time, between 10,000 and 40,000 years ago, many groups of people left Siberia in search of game and crossed the land bridge to Alaska. Descendants of these people are called Native Americans, or American Indians.

Some of the travelers passed through what became Alaska and continued southward into Canada and the Lower 48. Others stayed in the Alaska area. Two of Alaska's Indian groups, the Haida and the Tlingit, settled on the coast of the Alaska Peninsula.

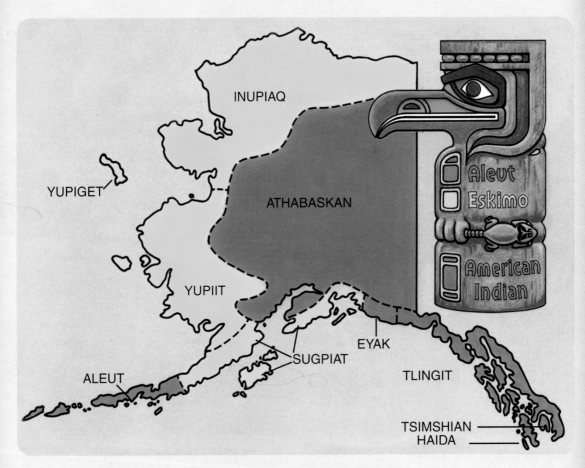

INUPIAQ

YUPIGET

ATHABASKAN

Aleut
Eskimo

American
Indian

YUPIIT

EYAK

SUGPIAT

ALEUT

TLINGIT

TSIMSHIAN
HAIDA

Alaskan Arrivals

The native people of Alaska consist of American Indians, Eskimos, and Aleuts. Groups of American Indians were the first people to live in Alaska. The Aleuts and the Alaskan Eskimos arrived years later. Today about 116,000 native people live in Alaska.

In front of their houses, the Native Americans raised huge, carved tree trunks called totem poles. As tall as telephone poles, the giant posts were carved with **totems**—images of plants and animals, such as frogs, ravens, and bears. Totems were believed to have magical powers.

The Athabaskans, another group of Native Americans, traveled in small bands throughout the central part of Alaska. During the short summers, the Athabaskans gathered berries and caught fish. In the winter, they strapped snowshoes onto their feet to make walking over deep snow easier. The Athabaskans hunted caribou, moose, and mountain sheep with snares or bows and arrows, or by corner- ing the animals in corrals.

Thousands of years after the Native Americans arrived, groups that came to be called the Alaskan Eskimos and the Aleuts arrived. These people made the journey from Siberia by boat, after the sea had covered the land bridge. The Alaskan Eskimos and the Aleuts settled mainly in coastal areas, hunting sea mammals for food and clothing.

Ancient Eskimos who lived near the Bering Strait buried these harpoon heads in graves.

Totems

The Haida and the Tlingit believed that certain animals had special powers. To represent these magical animals, the Indians made images called totems. The totems were linked to privileges, or rights, that were claimed by families or individuals. A totem might stand for the right to use a special name, to perform a dance during a ceremony, or to wear a particular mask.

Families displayed their totems in many ways, using them to decorate almost everything they owned. Some wove totems into blankets and clothing or painted them on boxes. Others carved the totems into spear and knife handles or made masks with totems. But the most well-known display of the images was the totem pole. Some totem poles illustrated a family's history or honored a dead family member. Others celebrated a special event. Totem poles with openings carved through them often served as entrances to homes. No matter how totems were displayed, they were always symbols of power.

From narrow boats called **kayaks,** Eskimo and
Aleut hunters harpooned seals, walrus, sea lions,
and sea otters. Oiled seal or walrus skins were
stretched over the boat's frame to keep cold water
from slopping into the hunter's lap. Each hunter sat
in the boat's cockpit—a hole cut into the deck.

Unlike the Eskimos in modern-day northern
Canada, Alaskan Eskimos and Aleuts did not live in
igloos, or houses made of snow and ice. Instead,
they built homes with stones, driftwood, whale ribs,
and blocks of earth and grass called sod. The dried
intestines of sea mammals were stretched over the
windows to keep out the cold and to let in sunlight.

The Aleuts used
one-person boats
called kayaks to hunt
and fish.

The first European explorer to set foot in what became Alaska was Vitus Bering.

Until the 1700s, Europeans had never met the Alaskan Eskimos and Aleuts or any of the American Indians in what came to be called Alaska. In 1724 Peter the Great, the czar (ruler) of Russia, decided to find out if any part of Siberia was connected to North America. The czar asked Vitus Bering, a Danish seaman, to travel by land to Siberia so he could set sail from the region's northeastern coast. In 1741, on their second journey, Bering and his crew found Alaska and proved that water completely separated North America from Siberia.

Bering's sailors returned to Russia with the pelts of sea otters, seals, and foxes—animals they had killed on the islands they visited. Siberian fur traders, eager to find new hunting grounds, headed for the region to collect furs.

Fur traders, able to earn huge profits selling pelts, soon swarmed over the Aleutian Islands, killing animals that the Aleuts depended on for food and clothing. The fur traders also stole furs from the Aleuts. Because the Aleuts were so skilled at hunting and boatbuilding, the fur traders forced Aleut

During the winter months, the Aleuts wore long coats and dresses made out of furs and skins.

men to hunt animals for them, while they held Aleut women and children hostage.

In 1784 a fur trader named Grigory Shelekhov established the first Russian settlement in North America, on Kodiak Island. From this settlement, Shelekhov thought he could control the fur trade in the area, which became known as Russian America.

Between 1807 and 1867, the town of Sitka was the capital of Russian America.

Shelekhov's plan worked. In 1799 the Russian government gave complete control of the Russian American fur trade to Shelekhov's Russian-American Company. Under the direction of Aleksandr Baranov, the Russian-American Company moved its headquarters to Sitka, on the Alaska Panhandle. Baranov took this land from the Tlingit Indians.

In retaliation, the Tlingit burned the Russian company's fort in 1802, killing most of the men and capturing the women and children. Two years later, the Russians attacked a Tlingit village near Sitka. The Tlingit fled but continued to attack Russian settlements for several years.

Although the Russian-American Company maintained several settlements, only about 800 Russians ever lived in Russian America. And by the 1860s, the Russian fur traders had killed so many sea otters and other fur-bearing mammals that the animals were becoming harder and harder to find. Russia decided to sell the land they called Russian America.

The Russian government had never bought the land from the Alaskan Eskimos, Aleuts, or Indians. But in 1867, Russia signed a **treaty** with the United States, selling Russian America for just over $7 million, or about 2 cents per acre. The United States called the new land Alaska, after the Aleut name for the area—*Alyeska*, which means "great land" or "main land."

Only 26 years after the Russians began hunting Steller's sea cows, they became extinct. Each of the sea cows weighed about 4 tons.

Because the few residents of Alaska lived so far from each other, the area earned the nickname the Last Frontier. The name meant it was an unknown and unsettled land. Alaska's vast wilderness would take years to explore, so it remained a true **frontier** for many decades.

In the first years that Alaska was part of the United States, churches sent **missionaries** to the Last Frontier. The missionaries wanted to teach the area's native people about the Christian religion and about the ways of life in the United States.

In 1867, officials replaced Sitka's Russian flag with the U.S. flag.

When white settlers arrived in Alaska, they changed native culture dramatically. For example, they encouraged native people to wear less traditional clothing.

Forced to live in missionary villages, the native people attended mission churches and boarding schools. The schools were designed to teach children to be more like white people. If students were caught speaking their native language, they were punished, sometimes with whips.

Like the Russian fur traders, many Americans saw Alaska as a place to make money. Companies from the Lower 48 liked working in Alaska because the local government didn't collect taxes or try to control businesses.

White hunters killed many whales and walrus, animals traditionally hunted by the Native Americans for food. The Native Americans were forced to raise reindeer for meat to supplement their diet.

One industry that grew quickly was fish canning. Alaska's first cannery was built in 1878. In 1890 the operations along just one river on Kodiak Island processed 3 million salmon. By 1898 Alaska's coast was home to more than 55 canneries. They made huge profits selling the fish to the Lower 48 and to other countries.

As the canneries processed more fish, some Alaskans worried that salmon and other fish would be killed off completely. But the canneries were powerful. They were able to prevent the U.S. government from passing laws to control how many fish were taken from Alaska's rivers and ocean waters.

Other people were more interested in gold than fish. In 1896 prospectors George Washington Carmack, Skookum Jim Mason, and Tagish Charley found gold in Bonanza Creek. Right across the border from Alaska, the creek ran into Canada's Klondike River.

The Klondike discovery excited people from all over the United States. The easiest way to reach the Klondike region was to travel by ship to Alaska and then to cross the mountains following overland trails. At least 100,000 people headed through Alaska for the Klondike, hoping to become rich by finding their own nuggets of gold. During the cold winters, many of the gold seekers were killed by freezing temperatures. Avalanches in the mountains of Alaska and of the Klondike region took the lives of other prospectors.

Those who came to Alaska during the gold rush risked their lives crossing rough terrain to reach the Klondike.

The gold in the Klondike encouraged prospectors to look for gold in Alaska, too. A few prospectors found the precious metal on the beaches of the Bering Sea in 1899. A shovel was all that was needed to scoop the gold out of the sand.

The town of Nome sprang up overnight as gold seekers rushed to the area. By 1900 Nome's population had climbed to 17,000, but most of the gold within easy reach had already been dug up. Only large mining companies with big, expensive equipment could continue to mine the area. Some of the town's residents opened stores, hotels, and other businesses to make a living.

In 1906 the U.S. government allowed Alaskans to elect a delegate, or nonvoting congressperson, to represent them in the nation's capital. Six years later, Alaska became an official U.S. territory. Many residents of the Last Frontier wanted that territory to become a state. The canneries and mining companies were against statehood. They feared the state government would pass laws that would limit their business activities.

Matanuska's Miracle

In the 1930s, the U.S. economy was in poor shape. Many men and women had lost their jobs or their farms. To deal with some of these problems—and to help Alaska's population grow—the United States government came up with a plan in 1935. The government offered to move about 200 hard-hit farm families to Alaska's Matanuska Valley. The families chosen for the project came from Michigan, Wisconsin, and Minnesota.

The first families arrived in Alaska in May 1935. They had no idea what to expect in what became known as the Matanuska Colony. High prices, no running water, and few tools made starting a farm difficult. Weeks of rainfall left the soil muddy and hard to work. Half of the newcomers gave up within three years.

Although other families replaced those who quit, the settlers continued to struggle through the 1940s. By 1950 the experiment was finally working. In modern times, 60 percent of Alaska's farm products come from the Matanuska Valley.

Settling in the Matanuska Valley gave struggling Midwestern farmers the hope of being able to care for their families without relying on charity.

By the early 1930s, only about 65,000 people were living in Alaska. Very few roads crossed the isolated territory, and no roads connected Alaska to Canada or to the Lower 48 U.S. states. People traveled and supplies were sent to and from the territory mostly by ship.

During World War II (1939–1945), the United States government built a highway in order to connect Alaska to the northernmost highways in Canada. Called the Alaska Highway, the road runs 1,397 miles from Delta Junction, Alaska, to Dawson Creek, British Columbia. About 9,000 soldiers and 12,000 workers constructed the entire road in less than a year.

The war itself came to Alaska, too. In June 1942, the Japanese bombed Dutch Harbor, a military base on the Aleutian Islands, and occupied two of the Aleutian Islands—Attu and Kiska. A year later, U.S. troops drove the Japanese off Attu. When Canadian and U.S. soldiers landed on Kiska Island later that summer, they found only two dogs. The Japanese had already retreated.

On June 3, 1942, Japanese forces attacked Dutch Harbor on the Aleutian island of Unalaska. Three days later, they occupied the island of Attu.

A Botched Evacuation

The United States became involved in World War II in December 1941, when the Japanese bombed Hawaii. By 1942 the Japanese had taken aim at bases in Alaska, too. In fact, the westernmost Aleutian island, Attu, was located only 600 miles from Japanese soil.

In June 1942, the Japanese attacked Attu and captured its Aleut population. To protect the remaining Aleuts, the United States government decided to evacuate (remove) them by force. The more than 800 evacuees had little time to collect their belongings before being sent to camps in southeastern Alaska.

Conditions in the camps were terrible. The buildings could not keep out the cold, and there were not enough toilets, beds, and medical supplies. Many older Aleuts died during the wartime evacuation.

After the war ended in 1945, the Aleuts were allowed to return home. Most found their belongings gone and their houses in ruins. In 1988 the U.S. government admitted that it had handled the evacuation badly. It offered the surviving Aleut evacuees an official apology and $12,000 each in damages.

Many of the soldiers and construction workers who came to Alaska during the war stayed. By the end of the war, Alaska's population had grown to 112,000. Many of the territory's residents continued to call for statehood for Alaska. On January 3, 1959, Alaska became the 49th state and the first new state since 1912.

In the years following statehood, Alaska saw a steady increase in its population. The growing population brought many changes to Alaska's wilderness and to the lives of its native people. Many newcomers began to clear and to build on the state's richest wilderness areas. As more new residents settled in the Last Frontier, the area's native people were pushed off more and more of their traditional homelands.

Sod homes with whale rib supports have provided shelter to Eskimos for hundreds of years.

In Alaska some native people still use traditional hunting and fishing techniques. Fishers catch salmon using fish wheel traps *(left)* and then dry the fish in the sun on racks *(below)*.

After losing much of the land they had depended on for hunting and fishing, the native people were left with few ways to provide food, clothing, and shelter for themselves and their families. Many of the native people lived in remote areas of the state where there were few jobs, schools, or doctors' offices. Most had little money, and many were in poor health.

37

In 1971 the U.S. government returned 44 million acres of land to the Alaskan Eskimos, Aleuts, and American Indians. The native people set up special organizations called corporations to manage the land. They spent the money they earned on health care, on schools, and to create new jobs.

In 1980 the U.S. government set aside more than 100 million acres of land in the Last Frontier for national parks, forests, and wilderness areas. That same year, the government gave special hunting and fishing rights to native people in these areas.

Questions about preserving Alaska's wilderness arose when oil was discovered in 1968 at Prudhoe Bay on the Arctic coast. Between 1974 and 1977, the Trans-Alaska pipeline was built for transporting the oil from Prudhoe Bay to the port at Valdez on Alaska's southern coast. From here, the oil is shipped to the Lower 48.

The pipeline has provided many jobs for Alaskans and has been a big boost to the economy. But it has also led to the risk of oil companies spilling oil while drilling for it or transporting it.

The zigzagging Trans-Alaska pipeline transports oil 800 miles across the Alaskan countryside.

In 1989 Alaskans' fears about oil pollution came true. The oil tanker *Exxon Valdez* ran aground near Valdez and spilled about 11 million gallons of oil into Prince William Sound, an inlet off the state's southern coast. The oil contaminated large parts of Alaska's coastline and killed hundreds of thousands of birds, fish, and other animals.

The Exxon Corporation spent about $2 billion on major cleanup work, which lasted until 1992. By 1999, 10 years after the spill, some oil remained on beaches, and wildlife had not fully recovered.

The 49th state faces difficult decisions in the years to come. Alaskans hope to find a way to keep mining and fishing jobs and still preserve the state's wildlife and natural beauty. In this way, the state can continue to live up to its nickname—the Last Frontier.

PEOPLE & ECONOMY

Mining, Museums, and Mushing

In some parts of Alaska, mail is delivered by airplane. That's because many small towns have no roads connecting them to the outside world. With so few people living in vast areas of the state, Alaska can't afford to keep up many roads. The Last Frontier counts less than two persons for every square mile.

JUNEAU   1300MI.

NOME   350MI.

ANCHORAGE 750 MI

KOTZEBUE   170 MI.

KIVALINA   75MI.

CAPE THOMPSON 30MI.

SIBERIA   200MI.

Alaskans traveling between cities have a long trip. This sign *(right)* alongside a road updates travelers on their progress. In the seaport town of Ketchikan *(facing page)*, wooden houses line the shore.

Anchorage hugs Alaska's southern coast. In 1964 the city was badly damaged by an earthquake.

But most Alaskans do have neighbors—and roads connecting them. About two-thirds of the state's 627,000 residents live in or near cities. Alaska's largest city, Anchorage, is home to almost half of the state's population. Next in size is Juneau—the state capital—with a population of about 30,700 people, and then Fairbanks, with 30,200 people in the city.

Native people make up about 19 percent of Alaska's total population. Three main groups— Eskimos, Aleuts, and Native Americans—live in

Alaska. Alaskan Eskimos are the largest group, with about 52,000 people. Within the Eskimo peoples are many groups. Most of the Inupiat live in the northern and western parts of the state. The Yupiit, Yupiget, and Sugpiat make their homes in the Pacific Mountains, on Saint Lawrence Island, and on Kodiak Island.

Young Alaskans find plenty to do in the great outdoors.

The Aleutian Islands and the Alaska Peninsula are home to many of the 8,000 Aleuts in Alaska. More than 24,000 other Native Americans—including the Haida, Tlingit, Athabaskans, Tsimshian, and others—live in different parts of the state.

Most of Alaska's non-native residents have European ancestors. Many of them moved north to the state from the Lower 48, and others arrived with the U.S. military. Some Alaskans came directly from Europe. Many of the residents of Petersburg, for example, are descendants of Norwegian fishers.

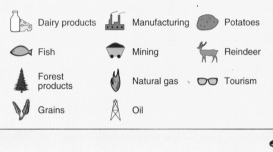

ALASKA
Economic Map

The symbols on this map show where different economic activities take place in Alaska. The legend below explains what each symbol stands for.

Dairy products		Manufacturing		Potatoes	
Fish		Mining		Reindeer	
Forest products		Natural gas		Tourism	
Grains		Oil			

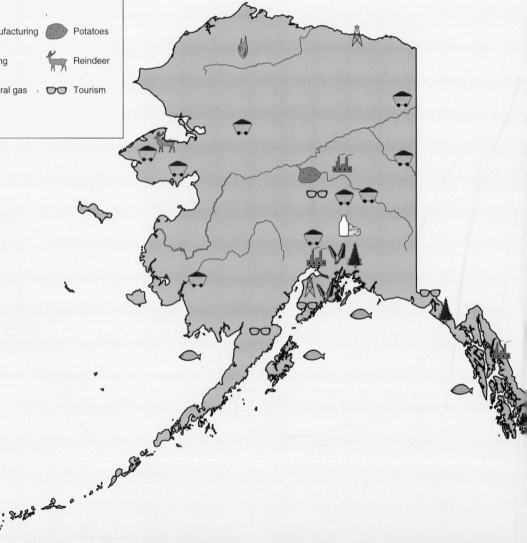

A fisher pulls crabs from a trap.

People in towns like Petersburg depend on the ocean to earn a living. Many Alaskans who live near the coast fish for salmon, crabs, halibut, herring, and shrimp.

Mining makes the largest amount of money for Alaska, and a vast majority of these earnings come from oil. Many companies drill for oil at Prudhoe Bay, one of the most active oil-producing regions in the world.

Mining companies also search for gold near Nome and Fairbanks. A large deposit of molybdenum, a metal used in making steel, is mined near Ketchikan. Alaskans dig up sand, gravel, and crushed stone to build roads. Coal, lead, silver, tin, zinc, and natural gas are also mined in Alaska.

At Alaskan sawmills and pulp mills, workers process timber into building materials and paper.

Many of Alaska's manufacturing jobs are tied to the state's mining and fishing industries. Alaskans work in canneries that clean and package the salmon, crab, herring, and other fish caught in

Alaskan waters. Other people work in oil refineries, where oil is processed to make petroleum products such as gasoline and plastic. Some Alaskans make paper and wood products from Alaska's timber.

The service industry employs the most Alaskans. A lot of service workers assist the tourists that visit the state. Other service workers teach in Alaska's schools or treat patients in the state's hospitals. Others have jobs as lawyers, salespeople, and news reporters.

A few Alaskans farm, especially in the fertile Matanuska Valley of central Alaska. On the state's 520 farms, Alaskans raise beef and dairy cattle, chickens, pigs, and sheep. Some Alaskan Eskimos raise reindeer for meat. Farmers also grow grains, fruits, and vegetables, such as wheat, cabbages, and potatoes.

The fur industry still provides jobs for some Alaskans. But most hunters no longer search for fur-bearing animals at sea. Instead, Alaskans trap land animals, including wolves, beavers, wolverines, lynx, marten, and mink.

Visitors to Sitka can take a tour of the old Russian settlement with guides dressed in traditional Russian clothing.

Traveling over mountains and through thick forests, the Alaska Railroad follows the state's coast.

Most of the roads in Alaska link cities such as Anchorage and Fairbanks to the Alaska Highway. Travelers also can catch one of the ferries that chug up and down Alaska's coastline, stopping at cities and towns on the Alaska Panhandle and along the state's southern coast. The Alaska Railroad carries people and supplies from the port at Seward to Anchorage and Fairbanks.

Air taxis are often the easiest way to travel through the Alaskan wilderness.

Alaska's airports, ferries, and roads bring about 1.1 million tourists to Alaska each year. Visitors have plenty to see and do. For example, they can learn about Alaska's history, its people, and its land at the state's museums.

In Sitka the Sheldon Jackson Museum—the oldest museum in the state—displays kayaks, dogsleds, masks, and other useful items made by Alaska's native people. Exhibits at the Alaska State Museum in Juneau feature everything from Russian culture in Alaska to wildlife and modern art. At the University of Alaska Museum in Fairbanks, displays show how gold and copper are mined, and visitors can see a three-ton copper nugget.

The Thrill of the Iditarod

The history of the Iditarod Trail Sled Dog Race begins in 1925. In that year, skilled sled drivers, called mushers, used teams of sturdy sled dogs to carry diphtheria vaccines from Anchorage to Nome. The vaccines saved many lives, and the dogs and drivers were considered heroes. In memory of the run, mushers set up a yearly race in 1973.

The mushers and their dogs prepare for the race year-round.

Mushers must know how to harness their dogs and how to cook the dogs' food. Drivers also have to be able to repair broken sleds and to tend their dogs if they are sick or injured.

The sled dogs are trained to follow the musher's commands. At the front is the lead dog, who guides the team down safe trails. Swing dogs make sure that the team and the sled stay on the trail, especially during hard turns. Team dogs use their strength to pull the sled. Nearest to the sled are the wheel dogs. Not only do these dogs get the sled going, but their calm attitude is just right for being so close to a moving vehicle.

Alaska is a haven for adventurers. Ice climbing *(below)* and white-water kayaking *(left)* are both popular sports.

One of Alaska's most exciting sports is dog mushing, or sled-dog racing. Every March dog teams compete in the Iditarod Trail Sled Dog Race, which covers a grueling 1,049-mile route from Anchorage to Nome.

Thousands of skiers, hikers, and climbers visit Alaska's wilderness areas each year. Skiers can whoosh down the slopes just outside downtown Anchorage. Or they can go by helicopter to the Juneau Ice Field and trek down one of Alaska's **glaciers.**

Hikers can follow the Chilkoot Trail—the old route of the Klondike gold prospectors—at Klondike Gold Rush National Historical Park near Skagway. Visitors may spot moose or Dall sheep wandering across the hiking trails of Alaska's many parks. Experienced climbers can try to reach the top of Mount McKinley in Denali National Park.

For people who enjoy water sports, Alaska's rivers offer the thrill of white-water canoeing, kayaking, and rafting. Anglers fish for trout and salmon. But anglers have to share their favorite fishing spots—salmon are also one of the favorite foods of bald eagles and grizzly bears!

Sometimes anglers reel in a surprise giant octopus.

THE ENVIRONMENT

Oil Spills and Wildlife

When the *Exxon Valdez* oil tanker ran aground in Prince William Sound in March 1989, 11 million gallons of oil gushed from the ship's hull, or body, where the oil was stored. The oil, drilled at Prudhoe Bay and carried by the Trans-Alaska pipeline to Valdez, was on its way to the Lower 48.

The oil spread across 3,000 square miles of ocean and washed up on more than 1,300 miles of beach along the Alaskan coast. After the spill, seabirds thought the dark patches of oil were schools of fish. The birds plunged through the oil to catch fish, and the oil coated their feathers, gluing them together. Without clean, fluffed feathers, the birds couldn't keep themselves warm in the ice-cold ocean waters.

Many animals died as a result of the oil spill. This bald eagle was one of the victims.

When the *Exxon Valdez* *(right)* struck a reef in Prince William Sound in 1989, other ships helped clear away the oil. But the spill was difficult to contain. Most of the oil washed onto the coast *(below)*.

Many oiled birds died from exposure to the cold. Others were poisoned by the oil—either by swallowing it as they tried to clean their feathers or by eating oil-contaminated fish. Some birds died when the oil soaked through their skin.

Scientists estimate that between 250,000 and 390,000 seabirds died. As many as 5,000 sea otters may have died, too, along with whales, bald eagles, harbor seals, salmon, and other animals and plants.

The Exxon Corporation was held responsible for cleaning up the oil. The cleanup crews tried several methods. Workers used **booms,** which look like big, floating logs, to surround the oil and keep it from spreading. Boats called **skimmers** were equipped with vacuums to suck up the trapped oil.

Along the contaminated coast, cleanup crews surround the oil with booms in an attempt to contain the spill.

The cleanup crews also tried using **dispersants**—chemicals that break up an oil slick into small droplets of oil. The droplets then disperse, or spread out, in the water, speeding up the natural decaying process of the oil. Dispersants help thin out oil slicks faster, but they also mix oil into the surrounding water, making it poisonous for fish.

Along the beaches, workers used peat moss, straw, and chemicals to soak up the oil. Workers also sprayed powerful jets of hot water to force the oil back into the water, where it could be picked up by skimmers. But this hot-water method killed marine creatures that could not survive in the high water temperatures. The water jets pushed oil under the sand and rocks and even deeper into the ground.

Workers use straw and heavy-duty paper towels to clean oily rocks on the beach.

Otters were also victims of the massive oil spill.

Another method tested by scientists from the Environmental Protection Agency (EPA) was to speed the growth of certain oil-eating bacteria on the beaches. The bacteria needed additional nutrients to be able to use the oil as food. So the EPA sprayed nutrient-rich fertilizer on the bacteria, causing them to grow and eat more and more of the oil.

After many months of cleaning up the oil, researchers and cleanup crews still couldn't tell how successful their efforts had been. In 1999, 10 years after the spill, there was still some oil on or near the surface of the water in parts of Prince William Sound. Beaches remained polluted, stopping residents and tourists from fishing, camping, and boating there. Populations of birds, fish, and other animals were not as great as they had been before the spill. But the numbers of river otters, bald eagles, and pink salmon were increasing. Many more years may pass before Alaskans know the long-term effects the oil spill has had on their environment.

People generally agree that the best way to protect Alaska's wildlife, beaches, and water from oil pollution is to stop oil from spilling in the first place. By using extra care in transporting oil, the operators of oil tankers can avoid oil leaks. To help prevent oil spills, some people want oil to be carried in ships that are built with two hulls—an inner one for oil storage and an outer one for protection. That way, if a tanker runs aground, only the outer hull is likely to crack, leaving the inner hull and the oil untouched.

Because millions of people depend on oil to heat their homes and fuel their cars, oil companies will probably not stop drilling for or transporting oil. But some people want oil exploration in Alaska to end. In particular, they don't want oil companies to drill in the Arctic National Wildlife Refuge on Alaska's northern coast. Oil companies want to drill in the refuge because they suspect it has vast amounts of oil hidden beneath the permafrost.

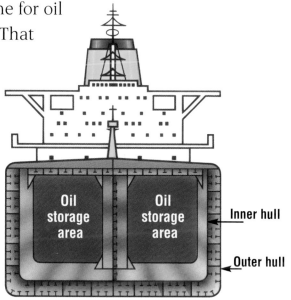

A double-hulled oil tanker

People in favor of leaving the refuge alone are afraid that drilling will threaten animals and people who live there. The refuge is home to large caribou herds and 200 other kinds of Arctic animals, such as polar bears and musk ox. Some native people in the area rely on the caribou for food and clothing.

People who want oil companies to drill in the wildlife refuge argue that oil is important to Alaska's economy. Since oil was discovered at Prudhoe Bay in 1968, the oil industry has provided thousands of jobs for Alaskans. Money raised by taxing oil companies is used to pay many government workers. The state's oil profits have allowed Alaska to stop collecting income taxes and to pay residents part of the money it earns from oil.

Oil is important to the U.S. economy, too. President George W. Bush and other leaders believe that using oil from the Arctic National Wildlife Refuge would reduce the amount of oil the United States buys from other countries and bring down the high price of oil. Alaska's oil would benefit the whole country, they argue.

Oil from Prudhoe Bay will eventually run out. For this reason, many Alaskans want the jobs and money that drilling the Arctic National Wildlife Refuge could bring. Alaskans who are against the drilling argue that if oil is found and drilled for in the refuge, it will likely run out someday, too. No one knows how much oil is under the refuge—there could be enough for several years, or just a few months. Sooner or later Alaskans will have to find other ways to earn money.

The U.S. government controls the Arctic National Wildlife Refuge and other wilderness areas in the state. Alaskans and other U.S. citizens can let the government know how they feel about drilling for oil in Alaska. Together, the people will decide if the risks to the environment are worth the oil, jobs, and money that come from drilling in the Last Frontier.

Many animals graze on the grasses and lichen that cover the Arctic National Wildlife Refuge.

ALL ABOUT ALASKA

Fun Facts

Although Alaskan summers are short, the sun shines about 20 hours each day and helps to produce enormous vegetables. Cabbages, for example, can grow to be as heavy as 90 pounds.

Alaska's yearly catch of fish is larger and worth more money than the catch of any other state in the nation.

Every year, more bald eagles flock to southeastern Alaska than to any other spot in the world. The fish-eating birds are attracted by easy-to-catch salmon that are swimming upriver.

Alaska has about 100,000 glaciers. Together, they cover about 29,000 square miles, or 5 percent of the state. Malaspina Glacier in Alaska is North America's biggest glacier. It is larger than the state of Rhode Island.

The world's longest chain of active volcanoes is in Alaska. Since the year 1700, at least 41 different volcanoes have erupted in Alaska. Some of them have blown up as many as 25 times.

An excursion ship carries passengers right up to an Alaskan glacier.

STATE SONG

"Alaska's Flag" is the only state song that focuses on a state flag. The song was first published in 1935, and it was adopted as Alaska's official state song in 1955.

ALASKA'S FLAG

Words by Marie Drake
Music by Elinor Dusenbury

Eight stars of gold on a field of blue, A-las-ka's flag, may it mean to you; The blue of the sea, the ev-'ning sky, The moun-tain lakes and the flow'rs near-by; The gold of the ear-ly sour-dough's dreams, The pre-cious gold of the hills and streams; The bril-liant stars in the north-ern sky, The Bear, "the Dip-per," and shin-ing high, The great North star with its stead-y light, O'er land and sea a bea-con bright, A-las-ka's flag to A-las-kans dear, The sim-ple flag of a last fron-tier.

You can hear "Alaska's Flag" by visiting this website:
<http://www.dced.state.ak.us/tourism/learn/learn19.htm>

AN ALASKA RECIPE

Alaska is a leader in the commercial fishing industry, and fishing fans flock to the state to catch salmon. Over a third of all wild salmon caught in the world each year come from Alaska's waters. If you can't go fishing yourself, you can find the salmon you need for this basic recipe in the supermarket.

BAKED SALMON RECIPE

You will need:

2 to 2½ pounds salmon fillet
¼ cup butter or margarine, melted
1 clove garlic, mashed or chopped
1 small onion, finely chopped
3 tablespoons parsley, finely chopped

2 tablespoons lemon juice
½ teaspoon sweet basil, crumbled
1 teaspoon salt
½ teaspoon freshly ground pepper

1. Have an adult preheat the oven to 300° F.
2. Place salmon fillet on piece of tin foil, to keep it from sticking to oven rack. Cut out foil around fish. Slide fish and foil onto rack of boiler pan.
3. Blend together remaining ingredients. Spread over fillet. Put fish into oven.
4. Bake for 25 to 30 minutes, depending on thickness of fillet. It's done when fish flakes when scratched with a fork.

Serves 8.

HISTORICAL TIMELINE

8000 B.C. American Indian groups are living in Alaska.

A.D. 1741 Vitus Bering lands on Alaska's coast and claims the region for Russia.

1784 Russia builds its first North American settlement on Kodiak Island.

1802 Fights over land rights begin between Tlingit and Russians.

1824 Russians agree to recognize 54° 40' as the southern boundary of Alaska.

1867 Russia sells Alaska to the United States.

1884 The U.S. Congress gives Alaska laws and a federal court.

1896 Prospectors find gold near the Klondike River.

1912 The U.S. Congress establishes Alaska as a U.S. territory.

1942 Japanese troops occupy two of the Aleutian Islands during World War II.

1943 The Alaska Highway is completed.

1959 Alaska becomes the 49th state.

1964 A severe earthquake destroys parts of south central Alaska on March 27.

1968 Oil is discovered in Prudhoe Bay.

1971 The U.S. government returns land to Alaskan Eskimos, Aleuts, and American Indians.

1977 The Trans-Alaska pipeline is completed.

1980 The U.S. Congress passes a conservation act that sets aside about one-quarter of Alaska for the National Park Service.

1989 The *Exxon Valdez* oil spill devastates Prince William Sound.

1992 Most of Prince William Sound is cleaned up.

1998 The Alaska Sea Life Center, funded in part by the *Exxon Valdez* settlement, opens in Seward, Alaska.

OUTSTANDING ALASKANS

Bob Bartlett

Vitus Bering

Susan Butcher

Nellie Cashman

Edward Lewis ("Bob") Bartlett (1904–1968) grew up in Fairbanks and became a gold miner, a journalist, and finally a U.S. senator. After fighting for Alaskan statehood, Bartlett championed the passage of health laws and was one of the first senators to oppose the Vietnam War.

Vitus Bering (1681–1741), a Danish-born navigator who worked for Russia, landed on the Alaskan coast in 1741. His explorations proved that water separated Asia and North America. Bering Sea, Bering Strait, and Bering Island are named after him.

Susan Butcher (born 1954), a skilled dog musher and trainer living near Eureka, Alaska, is the first person ever to win three Iditarod races in a row—in 1986, 1987, and 1988. She won again in 1990. Her racing ability and close relationship with sled dogs have made her a tough competitor.

Nellie Cashman (1844–1925), immigrated to the United States from Ireland when she was three years old. During the gold rush of the 1890s, she came to Alaska, where she staked claims, opened a restaurant, and ran a grocery store. She is remembered as the first white woman who dared to venture into the Klondike alone. The city of Seattle recognizes outstanding female business owners with an award named after Nellie.

Nora M. Dauenhauer (born 1927) spoke only Tlingit until she was eight years old and went to school. Her love of her native language has led her to collect, translate, and preserve the stories that Tlingit have long passed down by word of mouth.

Ernest Gruening (1887–1974), although trained as a doctor, became a journalist specializing in international affairs. In 1939 Gruening moved to Alaska to become territorial governor and worked hard for statehood. After Alaska became a state, he was elected to the U.S. Senate, where he campaigned for the rights of native people.

Ernest Gruening

Celia M. Hunter (born 1919) ferried military planes to U.S. bases during World War II. After moving to Alaska, she set up a wilderness camp and became active in efforts to protect Alaska's environment. In 1976 Hunter became president of The Wilderness Society, a national environmental organization.

Celia Hunter

Andrew Isaac (1898–1991) was chief of the United Crow Band for 59 years. Born in a trapping camp, Isaac honored the traditional ways of his people but also emphasized the value of education and helped to wage the war against drugs and alcohol among Alaska's native people.

Jewel (born 1974), also known as Jewel Kilcher, grew up in Anchorage and Homer. After high school the musician moved to California, where she lived in a van and performed in coffeehouses. Her work paid off when she released her album *Pieces of You* and her songs "Who Will Save Your Soul?" and "You Were Meant for Me" became popular. Jewel also writes poetry and has starred in movies.

Jewel

Victor Jory (1902–1982), born in Dawson City, Alaska, was an actor who became famous for his "bad guy" roles. He appeared in many films and television shows, including *The Adventures of Tom Sawyer, Gone with the Wind,* and "Ironside."

Victor Jory

Joseph Juneau

Sydney Laurence

Joe Redington

Howard Rock

Joseph Juneau (1826–1900), while in his fifties, discovered gold in Alaska's first major gold strike. According to tradition, Juneau cried when he struck his riches, either in joy or in sorrow at being too old to spend it. The capital city of Juneau is named after him.

Sydney M. Laurence (1865–1940) was a painter who, although born in New York, visited Alaska frequently throughout his later life and died in Anchorage. His paintings, which captured the beauty of the Alaskan wilderness, often featured Mount McKinley.

Dorothy Page (1921–1989) and **Joe Redington** (1917–1999) organized the first Iditarod race in 1967 to mark the 100th anniversary of the sale of Alaska to the United States. That first run covered only part of the historic Iditarod trail blazed by mushers in 1925. By 1973, when the trail had been fully cleared, the race crossed more than 1,000 miles and carried a prize of $50,000.

Leroy Parsons (1907–1989), the inventor of cable television, moved to Alaska in 1953 and by 1967 had installed the state's first cable system. The system, set up in Barrow, Alaska, allowed people living there to watch television for the first time.

Virgil Partch (1916–1984), a cartoonist, was born on Saint Paul Island, Alaska. After being fired by the Disney studios for participating in a strike, Partch began to sell his cartoons to newspapers and magazines, including *Newsweek* and *Time*. His famous signature, VIP, appeared on all his drawings.

Howard Rock (1911–1976), born in Point Hope, Alaska, was an artist before founding the *Tundra Times* in 1962. The newspaper voiced the concerns of Alaskan Eskimos and American Indians and helped to file the first lawsuits supporting native land claims.

Mark Schlereth (born 1966), the first Alaskan-born athlete in the National Football League, has played offensive lineman for the Denver Broncos since 1994. A dedicated lineman from Anchorage, Schlereth is nicknamed "Stinky" after an Alaskan food made from rotting fishheads.

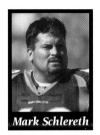

Mark Schlereth

Donald Simpson (1945–1996) was a film producer whose hit movies included *Flashdance*, *Top Gun*, and *Beverly Hills Cop*. The son of a hunting guide, Simpson was born in Anchorage.

Hudson Stuck (1863–1920) led the 1913 expedition that was the first to reach the tallest peak of Mount McKinley. He was better known as an Episcopalian missionary who fought to preserve the ways of Alaska's native people.

Donald Simpson

Innokenty Veniaminov (1797-1879) was a missionary for the Russian Orthodox Church. After he came to Alaska, he studied Native Alaskan languages and cultures. He devised an alphabet for the Aleut language. Veniaminov was designated a saint in 1977.

James Wickersham (1857-1939) was a judge when he came to Alaska in 1900. He served as a delegate to the U.S. Congress, where he introduced the first Alaska statehood bill and passed legislation to create Mount McKinley National Park. Wickersham also founded the college that later became the University of Alaska.

Hudson Stuck

Betzi M. Woodman (1913–1990), a daring news reporter for Reuters, gave the world its first eyewitness account of the severe earthquake that shook Alaska in 1964. Her prize-winning work took her to oil platforms, ice floes, and underground nuclear test sites.

Betzi Woodman

FACTS-AT-A-GLANCE

Nickname: Last Frontier

Song: "Alaska's Flag"

Motto: North to the Future

Flower: forget-me-not

Tree: Sitka spruce

Bird: willow ptarmigan

Land mammal: moose

Fish: giant king salmon

Mineral: gold

Sport: dog mushing

Date and ranking of statehood:
January 3, 1959, the 49th state

Capital: Juneau

Area: 591,004 square miles

Rank in area, nationwide: 1st

Average January temperature: 5° F

Average July temperature: 55° F

Alaska's state flag was designed by a 13-year-old Alaskan named Benny Benson. The flag features the Big Dipper and the North Star—famous stars that can be seen in the skies above Alaska. The blue background stands for the Alaskan sky and for the forget-me-not, Alaska's state flower.

POPULATION GROWTH

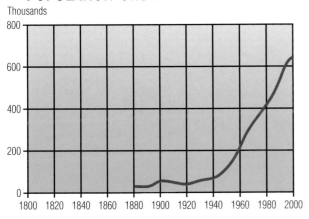

Thousands

This chart shows how Alaska's population has grown from 1880 to 2000.

Alaska's state seal was adopted in 1913. It depicts the northern lights, icebergs, and native Alaskan people. It also contains symbols of agriculture, fishing, and mining.

Population: 626,932 (2000 census)

Rank in population, nationwide: 48th

Major cities and populations: (2000 census) Anchorage (260,283), Juneau (30,711), Fairbanks (30,224), Sitka (8,835), Ketchikan (7,922)

U.S. senators: 2

U.S. representatives: 1

Electoral votes: 3

Natural resources: coal, fish and shellfish, forests, gold, gravel, natural gas, molybdenum, oil, sand, tin, water, zinc

Agricultural products: beef cattle, eggs, grains, greenhouse products, milk, potatoes, reindeer

Fishing industry: cod, Dungeness crab, flounder, groundfish, halibut, king crab, pollock, rockfish, sablefish, salmon, scallops, sea urchins, shrimp, smelt, tanner crab

Manufactured goods: construction materials, fish and seafood products, wood and paper products

WHERE ALASKANS WORK

Services—59 percent (services includes jobs in trade; community, social, and personal services: finance, insurance, and real estate; transportation, communication, and utilities)

Government—24 percent

Construction—5 percent

Manufacturing—5 percent

Agriculture and fishing—4 percent

Mining—3 percent

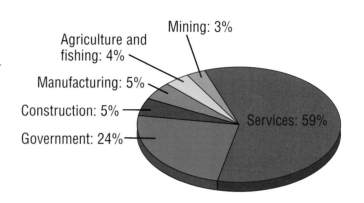

GROSS STATE PRODUCT

Services—47 percent

Mining—24 percent

Government—19 percent

Construction—4 percent

Manufacturing—4 percent

Agriculture and fishing—2 percent

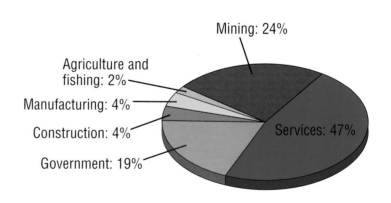

STATE WILDLIFE

Mammals: beluga whale, bison, black bear, Dall sheep, elk, fur seal, humpback whale, Kodiak brown bear, moose, musk ox, orca whale, polar bear, Sitka black-tailed deer, snow-white whale, walrus

Birds: arctic tern, bald eagle, blue grouse, boreal chickadee, Canada goose, common loon, emperor goose, golden eagle, gray jay, gyrfalcon, lesser golden-plover, lesser sandhill crane, merlin, snow bunting, snowy owl, tufted puffin, tundra swan, varied thrush, white-crowned sparrow, willow ptarmigan

Amphibians and reptiles: green sea turtle, leatherback sea turtle, spotted frog, western toad, wood frog

Fish: arctic grayling, crescent gunnel, cutthroat trout, dolly vardin, flounder, halibut, hooligan, king salmon, northern pike, Pacific herring, Pacific tomcod, pink salmon, sculpin, sockeye salmon, steelhead rainbow trout, walleye pollock, yelloweye rockfish

Trees: aspen, birch, black spruce, cottonwood, Sitka spruce, tamarack, western hemlock, white spruce, willow

Wild plants: arctic daisy, aster, bog laurel, cinquefoil, cowslip, firewood, forget-me-not, larkspur, lichen, moss, mountain laurel, sedge, violet, wild hyacinth, wood nymph

Bald eagle

PLACES TO VISIT

Alaska Native Heritage Center, Anchorage
The center is a great place to see re-created villages, craft demonstrations, dance performances, and historical displays of native groups from all over Alaska.

Alaska Sea Life Center, Seward
This is one of the top cold-water research and rehabilitation centers for marine wildlife.

Alaska State Museum, Juneau
Visitors to this museum can see Native American arts and artifacts, gold rush memorabilia, Russian relics, and wildlife displays.

Alaska Zoo, Anchorage
More than 50 species of native Alaskan birds and mammals can be seen at the Alaska Zoo.

Chilkat Bald Eagle Preserve, near Haines
Take a raft trip through this preserve. The best time to visit is between October and January, when more than 3,000 bald eagles come to the Chilkat River to feed on salmon.

Dog Mushing Museum, Fairbanks
Exhibits at the Dog Mushing Museum highlight Alaska's official state sport—dogsled racing. Watch videos of past races and view memorabilia and trophies.

Inside Passage, southeastern Alaska
Take a state ferry or cruise ship to see the beautiful blue-green water, abundant wildlife, and glaciers along this waterway.

Inupiat Heritage Center, Barrow
The star attraction at the center is a genuine *oomiaq*—a whaling boat made of wood and animal hide. Historical photos and artifacts of the Inupiat peoples are also on display.

Museum of History and Art, Anchorage
This museum features many Native American artifacts, arts and crafts, and fine art collections.

Inside Passage

University of Alaska Museum, Fairbanks
The museum displays pioneer relics, Native American artifacts, and Blue Babe, a 36,000-year-old preserved bison.

Valley of 10,000 Smokes, Katmai National Park and Preserve, Alaska Peninsula
The valley was named by Dr. Robert Griggs, who led a National Geographic Society exploration team through the valley in 1912. When Griggs first saw it, the valley was still smoking from the recent eruption of the Novarupta Volcano nearby. Although the valley no longer smokes, the wildlife is a sight to see.

ANNUAL EVENTS

Russian Christmas, statewide—*early January*

Iditarod Trail Sled Dog Race—*February or March*

Alaska Folk Festival, Juneau—*April*

Little Norway Festival, Petersburg—*May*

Salmon Derby, Sitka—*May*

Midnight Sun Festival, Nome—*June*

Sitka Summer Music Festival—*June*

World Eskimo Olympics, Fairbanks—*July*

Alaska State Fair, Palmer—*August*

Alaska Day Celebration, Sitka—*October*

Athabaskan Fiddling Festival, Fairbanks—*November*

LEARN MORE ABOUT ALASKA

BOOKS

General

Stefoff, Rebecca. *Alaska.* New York: Benchmark Books, 1998. For older readers.

Thompson, Kathleen. *Alaska.* Austin, TX: Raintree Steck-Vaughn, 1996.

Walsh Shepherd, Donna. *Alaska.* Danbury, CT: Children's Press, 1999. For older readers.

Special Interest

Blake, Robert J. *Akiak: A Tale from the Iditarod.* New York: Philomel Books, 1997. In this fictional tale, a sled dog named Akiak refuses to give up after suffering an injury during the Iditarod race.

Brown, Tricia. *Children of the Midnight Sun: Young Native Voices of Alaska.* Anchorage, AK: Alaska Northwest Books, 1998. Brown uses photographs and profiles to tell the story of Tlingit, Athabaskan, Yupik, and other Native American children in Alaskan cities, villages, and rural areas.

Corral, Kimberly. *A Child's Glacier Bay.* Anchorage, AK: Alaska Northwest Books, 1998. Corral relates the true story of an Alaskan family that takes a three-week sea kayaking trip along the Glacier Bay National Park and Preserve coastline.

Levinson, Nancy Smiler. *If You Lived in the Alaska Territory.* New York: Scholastic, 1998. This book describes what life was like for Eskimos living in Alaska Territory between 1912 and 1935.

McGinty, Alice B. *Sled Dogs: Speeding Through Snow.* New York: PowerKids Press, 1999. McGinty describes the history of dogsled racing and the work of sled dogs. Illustrated with color photos.

McMillan, Bruce. *Salmon Summer.* Boston: Houghton Mifflin, 1998. The author uses photographs to relate the story of a young Alaskan as he fishes for salmon on Kodiak Island.

Miller, Debbie S. *Disappearing Lake: Nature's Magic in Denali National Park.* New York: Walker and Company, 1999. This book describes the animal and plant life that thrives around a lake that only exists during the spring thaw.

Parker, Barbara K. *North American Wolves.* Minneapolis: Carolrhoda Books, 1998. Text and photographs introduce wolves, their habitat, their diet, and their way of life.

Rootes, David. *The Arctic.* Minneapolis: Lerner Publications Company, 1996. Rootes describes the region's landscape, the people who live there, and the natural and human threats to the Arctic's livelihood.

Staub, Frank. *Children of the Tlingit.* Minneapolis: Carolrhoda Books, 1999. This photo essay profiles Tlingit children who live in Alaska.

Wadsworth, Ginger. *Susan Butcher: Sled Dog Racer.* Minneapolis: Lerner Publications Company, 1994. A biography about Susan Butcher, a sled dog racer who won the Iditarod in 1986, 1987, 1988, and 1990.

Fiction

Willard, Tom. *Demons of Stony River.* Anchorage, AK: Publication Consultants, 1998. A story about Alaska's wolverines—some of nature's most fascinating animals.

WEBSITES

State of Alaska Online
<http://www.state.ak.us/>
Alaska's official website provides general information about the state's geography and landscape, and wildlife.

Alaska Division of Tourism
<http://www.dced.state.ak.us/tourism/>
Find out more about Alaska's most popular museums, festivals, and national parks at this informative website.

Anchorage Daily News
<http://www.adn.com/>
The online version of this newspaper is a great source for up-to-date news about Alaska.

PRONUNCIATION GUIDE

Aleut (al-ee-OOT)

Bering, Vitus (BEHR-ihng, VEE-tuhs)

Denali (duh-NAH-lee)

Haida (HY-duh)

Iditarod (eye-DIHT-uh-rahd)

Inupiat (in-OO-pee-at)

Juneau (JOO-noh)

Prudhoe (PROOD-hoh)

Sugpiat (SUHK-pat)

Tlingit (TLING-kuht)

Tsimshian (TSIM-shee-uhn)

Valdez (val-DEEZ)

Yupiget (yoo-PEE-khet)

Yupiit (yoo-PEET)

GLOSSARY

boom: a floating barrier placed around an oil spill to prevent it from spreading

dispersant: an agent that helps one substance to disperse, or scatter, into another substance

frontier: a part of a settled country that lies next to a region that is wilderness

glacier: a large body of ice and snow that moves slowly over land

kayak: a light Eskimo canoe that holds one person. The boat's wooden frame is covered with skins, except for a hole in the center for the kayaker.

missionary: a person sent out by a religious group to spread its religious beliefs to other people

peninsula: a stretch of land almost completely surrounded by water

permafrost: ground that remains frozen for two or more years. In Alaska, continuous permafrost occurs north of the Brooks Range and in high mountain regions.

precipitation: rain, snow, and other forms of moisture that fall to earth

skimmer: a boat equipped to pick up oil trapped by booms. Some skimmers have large ramps that scoop up the oil. Others have large vacuumlike hoses that suck up the oil.

totem: an animal or other object from nature taken by a family or tribe as its symbol. The images of totems decorate poles called totem poles.

treaty: an agreement between two or more groups, usually having to do with peace or trade

INDEX

PHOTO ACKNOWLEDGMENTS

Cover photographs by © Kevin Fleming/CORBIS (left) and © Paul A. Souders/COR-BIS (right); Digital Cartographics, pp. 1, 8, 9, 44; © Wolfgang Kaehler, pp. 2–3, 3; Harold Wahlman pp. 4 (detail), 7 (detail), 16, 19 (detail), 41 (detail), 53 (detail); NE Stock Photo: © Jim Schwabel, pp. 6, 51 (left), © Peter Cole, p. 12, © Grant Klotz, pp. 45, 46, 51 (right); Hodgens' Photography, p. 7; Root Resources: © Alan G. Nelson, p. 10, © Kenneth W. Fink, p. 36, © Ruth Smith, p. 40; Lynn M. Stone, pp. 11, 14 (both), 48, 49, 73; Visuals Unlimited: © Steve McCutcheon, pp. 13, 41, © Will Troyer, pp. 54 (bottom), 80; Kent & Donna Dannen, p. 15; © G. W. Biedel/Laatsch-Hupp Photo, p. 17; Jerry Hennen, pp. 18, 37 (both); IPS, pp. 19, 21 (both), 26, 31, 47; Betty Groskin, p. 22; AK and Polar Regions Dept., Univ. of AK Fairbanks: Rare Book Coll. (acc. #60024), p. 23, Klerekoper Coll. (acc. #77-158-178), p. 67 (top), Barrett Willoughby Coll. (acc. #72-116-413), p. 68 (second from top), Charles E. Bunnell Coll. (acc. #73-66-217N), p. 69 (second from bottom); AK State Library, Early Prints of AK Coll., pp. 24, 66 (second from top, bottom PCA 01-4024); Library of Congress, pp. 25, 66 (top); Stock Montage, p. 28; Smithsonian Institution (photo #75-5355), p. 29; Glenbow Archives, Calgary, Alberta (neg. # NC1-890), p. 30; Brown Brothers, Sterling, PA, p. 33; AK at War Coll., Univ. of AK Anchorage, Archives & Manuscripts Dept., p. 35; Adam Lerner, p. 39; © Kevin Fleming/COR-BIS, p. 42; © Paul A. Souders/CORBIS, pp. 43, 66 (second from bottom); Nancy Budrow, p. 50; Paul Ashner, p. 52; Bruce Batten, U.S. Fish and Wildlife Service, p. 53; Mike Lewis/ADEC, p. 54 (top); Oil Spill Public Information Center, p. 55 (top); Erich Gundlach/ADEC, p. 55 (bottom); 3M/Occupational Health & Environmental Safety Div., p. 56; © Scott T. Smith, p. 59; Jack Lindstrom, p. 60; Mary Ney, p. 61; Tim Seeley, pp. 63, 71, 72; Kathy Kilmer, p. 67 (second from top); © Mitchell Gerber/CORBIS, p. 67 (second from bottom); Hollywood Book & Poster, pp. 67 (bottom), 69 (second from top); Dictionary of American Portraits, p. 68 (top); John S. Foster, p. 68 (second from bottom); *Tundra Times*, p. 68 (bottom); ©Allsport USA/Brian Bahr; p. 69 (top); Lyman L. Woodman, p. 69 (bottom); Jean Matheny, p. 70 (top); © Chris Rainier/CORBIS, p. 75.